Seriously Bad Baby Names

by Chris Okum

*That which we call a rose
by any other name would smell as sweet;
but we're not naming roses.*

Book Design by Roy Fox

This book is going to save your child's life.

But before I continue, I think you should know that I had to scrap my original introduction, which was to be much more philosophical and indicative of my compulsion to come across as a real deep thinker, which I assure you I am not, and to prove this, let me point out that at this moment, as I type, I cannot stop thinking about a pair of shoes I am going to buy with the check I receive from writing this book. The shoes are hand-stitched, all buttery black leather, and on the bottom of the shoes are words that appear to be written in Italian. I just can't wait.

My original introduction was inspired by a paper titled Halo of Identity: The Significance of First Names and Naming, by M.D. Tschaepe of Gonzaga University. I use the word "inspired," but what I mean to say is that I highlighted what I thought were some prescient passages and was prepared to pass them off as my own. Some of the highlights included:

"Just as the object is brought into existence through naming, thereby becoming the name, so too the individual becomes its name; the name determines what the individual is." [i] [i]

And

"The first name, when placed within the individual, becomes a dictum that states, 'You are this' and 'You are that.'" [ii] [ii]

These are things I wish I had said, but I am not a Gary, or a Stan, or a William, or one of the myriad names that comes with it the ability to synthesize such ideas. No, I am a Christopher, and, as my name would indicate, am only able to scratch the surface of things, to glean what is most trivial and repeat it back ad infinitum, like a theme park

---

[i] [i] Tschaepe, M.D. Halo of Identity: The Significance of First Names and Naming (Janus Head, 6 (1)) 2003. 67-78.
[ii] [ii] Ibid.

automaton that teaches remedial American history to a room full of glassy-eyed tourists.

My name is my prison. Escape is pointless. If I were to escape my name, who would I be? Would I know how to speak? Ask for a sandwich? Would I know what a sandwich was? Without a name, people would not have a frame of reference by which to judge me.

And that's what this book is about; names, and what's going to happen to your child if you choose one of the names that graces the pages of this book. Most of the names I've chosen are fairly egregious, saddled with connotations that could, later in life, lead your child down a path strewn with dirty needles.

While compiling names for this book, I purposely shied away from the obvious. After all, no one needs to be told why naming a boy Adolf is not a good idea.

Every name bears the weight of every person who has ever had that name and all the things they did, good or bad, while the proprietor of that name, so while deciding a name for your child, think about what kind of person you want them to be, and think of the name you give them as the vehicle that will take them to that person.

In other words, the names in this book are lemons.
Consider yourself warned.

Chris Okum
Los Angeles, California
January, 2008

ARNOLD

Origin: **Teutonic**

Meaning: **Eagle power**

Famous Arnolds: **Palmer, Schwarzenegger**

It's hard for a boy to have self-esteem if his name is Arnold.

So you'll just have to excuse him when he moves back home shortly after his thirtieth birthday. But don't feel sorry for the baby that you named Arnold. He thinks that he deserved to be punished, especially after what he did to the turtles at the aquarium.

AGNES

Origin: **Greek**

Meaning: **Chaste**

Famous Agnes': **Moorehead, DeMille**

No matter how many times you tell Agnes why you named her Agnes she's never going to remember, because all Agnes' suffer from severe short-term memory loss.

This means that she's not going to remember your name too, a problem that can be remedied by wearing a name tag. How you're going to remind Agnes to look at the name tag is a problem for which there is no solution, at least not right now, although there are people with fancy degrees working on this as we speak, and who these people are I can't remember. My name is not Agnes, but then again, maybe it is.

A

BURT

Origin: **Teutonic**

Meaning: **Bright, Shining**

Famous Burts: **Reynolds, Lancaster, Bacharach**

Burt is what you name a boy who will one day grow up to be a square-jawed, broad-chested, take-no-prisoners He-man. Selfish with the fruits of his labor, Burt always has his eye on a prime piece of real estate, somewhere secluded, with plenty of space for his Armada of Stallions or collection of topless, custom-made luxury sedans, all of them adorned with Burt's signature logo, the lightning bolt.

B

BRENDA

Origin: **Scandanavian**

Meaning: **Sword**

Famous Brendas: **Vaccaro, Starr**

Brenda's a great name if you're the head spokesperson for a socially-conscious, politically-active organization

...wearing a caftan, barking orders through a megaphone, marching through the garment district, fist in the air, a tiny little lit professor in tweed pajamas waiting for you at home, the last time you saw him he was sitting in bed, grading papers, and as you shut the door he said, "meet you at the sheets," which is what you plan on doing as soon as you feel the media has heard your ten-point plan, but that's never going to happen, because that world is gone, it's not coming back, and it took the name Brenda with it.

B

CLYDE

Origin: **Scottish**

Meaning: **From the river**

Famous Clydes: **Barrow, Drexler**

Clyde has always felt that he didn't have anything interesting to say, but that doesn't mean he's not worth talking to.

Proficient in the art of light chat, Clyde is available to meet at various communal appliances (copy-machine, water cooler, coffee maker, microwave) and discuss the latest existential banalities. Is there a cutting-edge band that you're keen on checking out at the hottest new local art gallery? Clyde likes them and wishes he could go to the show, but he'll see them next time. Is it your birthday? It's Clyde's birthday too! And don't worry about not inviting Clyde to your scrumptious raw-food dinner bash where all your closest friends will usher you out of the coveted 18-34 demographic; Clyde's always the new guy at wherever he happens to be working, and, to be honest with you, if he was throwing a party there's a good chance that he wouldn't even invite himself. Not getting enough exercise? Well, neither is Clyde, even though he's ready to make the commitment, he's really going to try hard to lose ten to fifteen pounds, his face didn't always look like this, at one time he was quite a good athlete, well, not that good, I mean, it's not like he could've played in college. And what about traffic? Is traffic driving you crazy? It didn't always used to be like this and Clyde remembers a time when he could drive from here to there in lickety split. Clyde rarely speaks for more than a couple of seconds at a time, giving him plenty of opportunities to nod his head at your hard-earned life lessons and cackle at what he presumes to be stabs of humor. When you walk away from Clyde you'll always feel satisfied. Clyde, on the other hand, will be certain that he must've said something wrong.

C

CLORIS

Origin: **Latin**

Meaning: **Pale, Green**

Famous Cloris': **Leachman**

If you've decided to name your baby Cloris, there is a good chance you lack the patience necessary to get through an entire baby-naming book.

But you really need to soldier on, because there are some good names out there, names that fit perfectly with who you're baby is going to be, and Cloris is not one of them, unless you're baby is going to grow up to be the head nurse at a hospital for the criminally insane. Which could be what you want. I hear it's a very rewarding job that puts a lot of things in perspective, like the fact that your mother named you Cloris.

C

DENNIS

Origin: **Greek**

Meaning: **The God of wine**

Famous Dennis': **the Menace**

Being a Dennis is hard work.

At least twice a month every Dennis is expected to take an updated version of the classic Rosenzweig Picture-Frustration Test, in which all Dennis' are asked to look at a series of drawings that depict two people in a stressful situation. Over one of the crudely drawn characters there is a speech bubble in which an aggressive question is asked, such as "Why are you growing a beard during the middle of a heat wave?" It is Dennis' job to supply the answer in the second speech bubble. An aggressive answer, such as "Men with beards are frightening and I want people to leave me alone," on more than sixty percent of the pictures is indicative of a failing score, thus consigning Dennis to another two weeks as proprietor of their inanely passive first name. A passing score would allow any Dennis to pick a new first name. Although no Dennis has ever passed the Rosenzweig Picture-Frustration Test, an unofficial poll has been taken and it has been determined that ninety-percent of all Dennis', if given the choice, would like to change their name to Jesse.

D

DAWN

Origin: **English**

Meaning: **A first appearance; a beginning**

Famous Dawns: **Wells, Staley**

We get it. The birth of a baby is like the arrival of a new day, a chance to begin again, a clean slate, blah, blah, blah. You want to know what people really think about when they hear the name Dawn? Split ends.

Burgundy pant suits that smell like a pack of Virginia Slims. Scoliosis. Ringworm. Maybe these things don't describe your Dawn, but people will assume that they do, and in the end, isn't that all that matters? Don't you care what people think? Quick: ask the person next to you what they think of when they hear the name Dawn. See. I knew it.

D

EUGENE

Origin: **Greek**

Meaning: **Well Born**

Famous Eugenes: **O'Neill, Debs**

All current Eugenes were created by a Xerox-funded laboratory at Stanford during the early 70's.

At the time, the name Eugene was thought to be in danger of becoming extinct. The Original Eugene, also known as Eugene One, has over 3,000 copies, most of them living in small coastal towns were humid air is plentiful, as any given Eugene is prone to all manner of bronchial misadventure. Strangely enough, it is hard to find two Eugenes that get along, as each feels he is an improvement over the preceding Eugene, a notion that is usually challenged when two or more Eugenes come into contact.

ESTHER

Origin: **Hebrew**

Meaning: **Star**

Famous Esthers: **Rolle, Williams**

I don't mean to frighten you, but something bad is going to happen if you pick the name Esther.

Or at least that's what Esther's going to think, because Esther is the classic hypochondriac name. Every cough, every sniffle, every fever will be seen as evidence that Esther has caught a rare and cure-resistant disease, like small pox, or tuberculosis, one of those old-timey sicknesses that can only be contained for long enough so that the patient has the time to watch themselves wither away. But there's nothing wrong with Esther. Or maybe there is. You just never can tell with an Esther. One day, however, there will be something wrong with her, and then you'll see.

E

FRED

Origin: **Germanic**

Meaning: **Peaceful ruler**

Famous Freds: **Flintsone, Astaire**

It's not a good idea to name your son Fred. He will be made fun of by boys twice his size.

Fred, due to the working-class connotations of his name, will not take these japes lightly, and such as these things go, bones will be broken, all of them Fred's. These beatings will thin Fred's skin until it becomes like philo dough, at which point even the slightest hint that someone is mocking his name will send him into whirling fits of tight white rage. It will eventually be in everyone's best interest to adopt a neutral tone when speaking to Fred. In other words, pretend you're from Switzerland.

F

FERN

Origin: **English**

Meaning: **Young Deer**

Famous Ferns: **See below**

There are no famous women named Fern. I checked.

There is a woman named Fern Rhein, and according to the Hermosa Beach Historical Society of Hermosa Beach, California, she is famous, but only in relation to Hermosa Beach, which is kind of like being the deadest person in a cemetery.

GRANT

Origin: **French**

Meaning: **Great; tall**

Famous Grants: **Wood, Goodeve**

Say the name Grant out loud and it sounds like you're doing an impression of a bird that has wings but no idea what to do with them. This name is one of the main causes of noise pollution.

Wouldn't the world be a much more peaceful place if we didn't ever have to hear this name again? On a chart detailing which sounds pack the most decibels, the name Grant is right below a common household blender on permanent frappe. This is about what kind of world you want to live in, and most people would like to live in a Grant-free world, where someone's name doesn't cause them to flinch.

G

GLORIA

Origin: **Latin**

Meaning: **Gloria**

Famous Glorias: **Steinem, Estefan, Gaynor**

There has never been one documented case of a Gloria arriving on time for an important event, and that includes weddings, births, and funerals.

A natural flake, Gloria most likely will possess a hideous sense of direction and the inability to get dressed without throwing a I-Need-A-New-Wardrobe pity party. She will take left-overs without finding out who has called dibs, and sit at the head of the table when attending dinner parties she has not been invited to. There are those who will call her vulgar, but Gloria can't help but disagree and call herself eccentric, which would be fine if she didn't have potato salad and chopped liver in her hair when she says it.

G

HAROLD

Origin: **Scandanavian**

Meaning: **Army ruler**

Famous Harolds: **Bloom, Lloyd**

Harold is a real schlep name, the type of small-time actuary who leaves his wife and kids for a woman he's met at an airport bar.

Oh, he's getting a divorce alright, and once he does he's going to make sure he takes care of his blue-ribbon chippy, get her out of that apartment she's living in, the one catty corner from the local sports arena. Harold is a name dripping with desperation, the kind of name that no matter how hard you ring it still manages to be slightly damp the next day.

H

HILARY

Origin: **Greek**

Meaning: **Cheerful**

Famous Hilarys: **Clinton, Duff, Swank**

It's hard for a Hilary to have a nickname.

Hil? Hils? Lary? Nothing seems to fit. And these are just the beginning stages of a nickname. First you shorten, then you expand. But no one wants to expand unless they've shortened. So it will always remain Hilary, and Hilary will always remain on the outside looking in, certain that she could have been one of a kind if only her name wasn't so rigid and unforgiving.

IVAN

Origin: **Russian**

Meaning: **Believer in a gracious God**

Famous Ivans: **Boesky, The Terrible**

Ivan's a good name if you happen to be a drug dealer who lives in Warsaw.

If that's your name then it makes sense why you would want to burn down an apartment building. Go ahead and park your car in a handicap space. If someone asks you why you did it just tell them your name is Ivan, they'll understand. Some names are aromatic, bring with them a flood of memories, and Ivan is one of those names, it's very utterance conjuring up all manner of mayhem and panickey fright. This is a good name for your son if you can't afford a gun or a pit bull.

I

ILENE

Origin: **Greek**

Meaning: **Light**

Famous Ilenes: **None**

This is what you name your daughter when you want to impress the people you can't stand.

They talk about books you've never read, listen to repetitious music, and act as if nothing has or ever will shock them out of their belief that everything is and always will be the same. And then you come along with Ilene, a name so completely banal that no one even noticed it was available to use. Your adversaries recoil in horror at the sound of your child's name, then scatter and head for their lofts. A decisive battle has been won, but at what cost?

I

JIM

Origin: **Hebrew**

Meaning: **He who supplants**

Famous Jims: **Jones, Baker, Brown**

Jim, for all intents and purposes, is just another name for Dennis, except Jim has a beard.

But don't be fooled by the beard. Jim also must pass an exam once a month, one that's a little more complicated, involving a kite, a peanut butter and jelly sandwich with the crusts cut off, a stuffed squirrel, and a guitar made out of aluminum foil. Jim has only five minutes to figure out what the connection is between the four items, even though, unbeknownst to Jim, there is no connection, just as there is no connection between his name and any good reason for having his name, other than it just sounded like a good name for him to have. There has never been a Jim who has understood that the lack of connection is the connection, just as there has never been a Jim who has gotten the opportunity to change his name to Lance.

J

JOYCE

Origin: **Latin**

Meaning: **Merry**

Famous Joyces: **Oates, Brothers**

Joyce will drop by without calling, use all your toilet paper, and make you drive hours for a special hot dog that keeps her homesickness at manageable levels.

The third-leading cause of depression in women age 18-34 is having a friend named Joyce. There is an urban legend currently circulating around Dayton, Ohio that a young girl named Joyce once flushed herself down the toilet and now roams the sewers of the city, pasty and malnourished, talking to herself in the dark, asking if anyone knows where she can find some floss. You have better odds of winning the lottery than meeting a Joyce who is not wearing a black turtleneck sweater.

J

KIRK

Origin: **Scandanavian**

Meaning: **Believer**

Famous Kirks: **Douglas**

A great name for a pathological liar. You could catch Kirk stealing money out of your purse and he would tell you that he was just looking for some gum. The wallet could be in his hands and he would still tell you that he was just holding it because it was making it hard for him to find the gum. And what's the point of punishing a Kirk? How can you scream at a Kirk, when saying the name Kirk is just so darn pleasant? You can't. That's why he's going to get away with everything.

KAY

Origin: **Latin**

Meaning: **Fun-loving**

Famous Kays: **Boyle, Francis**

A short name means less letters, hence a lighter child, therefore don't be surprised when Kay is walking at six weeks, running at two months, and doing home gymnastics at a year.

You won't even know if Kay turned out to be a pretty little girl because all you'll ever see of her is flying elbows, tucked knees, and a head that's always upside down. Baby-proofing isn't even an adequate description for what you're going to have to do to where you live. Remember those blue mats for P.E. class, the ones that always seemed to be coated in a blanket of grit? Picture those mats wall to wall, floor to ceiling. No more tchochkes or tables for the tchochkes. As a matter of fact, say good-bye to furniture in general. Get used to sleeping on a pommel horse.

LEVI

Origin: **Latin**

Meaning: **Worshipful**

Famous Levis: **Strauss**

Most men named Levi are light as a feather, more concerned with trivial aspects of their own personal hygiene than making good on the biblical promise of their moniker.

As such, it is best to keep all tools away from a Levi, especially wrenches and pliers, which they often mistake for an exotic type of nail clipper. Levi is also worthless when it comes to automobile maintenance, known to emit a blood curdling shriek whenever a hood is popped in their vicinity. Oil and other viscous fluids are to Levi as Holy Water is to the Vampire. Levi would be working for the weekend if working didn't make him sweat so much, especially since he's always wearing linen.

L

LYNN

Origin: **English**

Meaning: **Fresh as spring water**

Famous Lynns: **Redgrave, Cheney**

Lynn will be an over-achiever, so don't be surprised when she files for emancipation at age 15, thus beginning her rapid ascent up the corporate ladder. She will spend the rest of her life telling anyone who will listen that she has no idea where she got her drive and ambition from, that these traits must not be hereditary. This will usually garner a big laugh, but not as big as the one she gets for doing an impression of you trying to open a childproof bottle of aspirin, complete with multiple well-timed and perfectly executed pratfalls, for she is the consummate performer, something that, once again, she did not learn from you.

L

MORTON

Origin: **English**

Meaning: **Sophisticated**

Famous Mortons: **Downey, Subotnick**

It's not nice to name your son Morton.

There's never been a leader of men named Morton. With a name like Morton, expect to be the mother of a despised bureaucrat, the type who thinks being a city councilman is reason enough to be drunk on power. Don't be surprised when your Morton gets busted, his bad name dragged through the mud by a local investigative news teams doing a b series of reports on illegal cockfights held in the backrooms of Chinese restaurants.

M

MELINDA

Origin: **Latin**

Meaning: **Sweetheart**

Famous Melindas: **Gates**

Out of all the names in this book I would have to give this one a vote for the absolute worst.

Melinda, for me at least, is a name that evokes nothing. It is a name without qualities.

I picture a face without eyes, without a nose, without a mouth. In other words, silly putty with a wig.

NICK

Origin: **Greek**

Meaning: **Winner**

Famous Nicks: **Nolte, Drake, Cave, Cage, Carter**

Nick has a long history of being a winner's name, but a losing streak is due, and the odds are that it will start with your son.

Forget a lifetime of brushed suede clothing, long silky locks, and hairpin turns executed in tiny Italian sports cars. Your Nick most likely has a future filled with endless speech therapists (he's going to have a lisp) and early male pattern baldness. I know that when you hear the name Nick there's a smoky sax playing somewhere in the distance, but listen closely, because in the case of your son, I hear nothing but a flute.

N

NORMA

Origin: **Latin**

Meaning: **Gold standard**

Famous Normas: **Kamali, Rae**

At first, Norma is going to think her name is a practical joke.

When she finds out it's not, the joke's going to be on you, because Norma's going to move to El Paso and get a job serving flapjacks in a diner next to a gas station, as that will be the only place that seems to go with her name. Yes, she'll come home to visit, and that's when you better sleep with one eye open, because payback is a dish best served cold in the middle of the night.

ORVILLE

Origin: **French**

Meaning: **Gold town**

Famous Orvilles: **Redenbacher**

Your job as a parent is to raise a child who decreases the circulation of sadness in the world. Naming your son Orville, it would seem, totally defeats this purpose.

OCTAVIA

Origin: **Latin**

Meaning: **Born on the eighth day of the month**

Famous Octavias: **Butler**

The perfect name for a child born on another planet. But guess what? She's not going to be living on another planet.

She's going to be living on this planet. And on this planet there are people who don't want to be reminded about the failed promise of space travel. Her name is like a taunt, almost a curse. It's saying, Hey pal, you're never getting off this giant spinning muddy rock, we tried, it didn't work, so you better settle in and think about how you want to redecorate. Inside the hushed, sterile halls of NASA, the person who utters the name Octavia has to leave the premises, drive to the nearest body of water, spin in a circle seven times, spit into their palm, and light an entire box of matches before they are allowed to be anywhere near the Space Shuttle.

O

PHILLIP

Origin: **Greek**

Meaning: **Lover of horses**

Famous Phillips: **McGraw, Mickelson**

Each Phillip has moveable hands and legs and comes with three interchangeable heads, each with it's own distinct expression: irritated, mad, and totally pissed off.

Dressed in saddle shoes (feels like real leather!), knee high socks, knickers, Dutch Boy shirt w/ red scarf, and beanie (spin the propeller!), Phillip can be posed successfully in almost any environment, although nothing suits him best like The Messy Bessy Kitchen PlaySet. Removable ice cream cone not included.

P

PEGGY

Origin: **Greek**

Meaning: **A pearl**

Famous Peggys: **Lee, Lipton**

Peggy is a smoker's name, at least three packs a day.

She's going to start her last year of elementary school and not decide to quit until she's had her own kids, by which time it will be too late, because motherhood is going to make her want to smoke even more. Peggy is a natural born melancholic. She'll try and discipline her children, but she'll feel funny about it considering that she can't even discipline herself. Peggy has phantom pain from missing teeth and her biggest fear is that she will fall overboard while on a cruise ship and wash up on the shores of a lost continent that does not harvest tobacco. Most of all, Peggy feels the constant need to apologize, but she doesn't know for what.

P

Now you're just trying too hard.

RANDY

Origin: **English**

Meaning: **Wolf counselor**

Famous Randys: **Johnson, Mantooth, Savage**

Randy wants to know if you think his hair looks good.

Otherwise he's not going out. When Randy walks into a crowded arena he wants to lead with his widow's peak. Not only does Randy's self-esteem emanate from his 'do, so does his future. Great hair equals jet skis and solid outings at the buffet. Bad hair equals a lifetime of drywall and the distinct possibility that he will be one of the few people, percentage-wise, who dies during a minor earthquake. One time Randy changed stylists and arrived at a friend's wedding with sweatstains on the back of his pants. Some would say there is no connection, but Randy knows that life hangs in the angle of the snip.

R

REBA

Origin: **Hebrew**

Meaning: **Fourth-born**

Famous Rebas: **MacIntyre**

Fact: In the lumber industry, a felled Sequoia is known as a "Reba".

Fact: According to a spokesperson for the Malibu Police Department, to be assaulted with a chaise lounge is "to have just had brunch with Reba."

Fact: In the medical community, surgeons who have lost the ability to keep a steady hand suffer from "Maladie de Reba."

Fact: Reba is an anagram for Bear.

Fact: "Reba" is the sound your refrigerator makes when you open the freezer.

Fact: Reba was what John Wilkes Booth named his revolver.

Fact: In the Republic of Yemen it is customary for the oldest son to make a pilgrimage across the Red Sea in a rowboat while blindfolded, otherwise known as the "Eid al-Reba."

SIDNEY

Origin: **French**

Meaning: **Attractive**

Famous Sidneys: **Sheldon, Poitier, Vicious**

Sidney comes with instructions.

Number 1: Squeeze his right hand until you see that his eyes are open. He should blink three times. After the third blink, he will close his eyes. If he does not blink three times this may indicate that his hand was not squeezed hard enough. If this should happen, please continue on to Number 7. Number 2: As soon as Sidney is done blinking, squeeze his left hand five times, followed by five squeezes to his right hand. It is now safe to say your name. If Sidney repeats your name, please continue on to Number 4. If Sidney does not repeat your name, please contact a customer service representative as you have given birth to a Sigmund instead.

SHARON

Origin: **Hebrew**

Meaning: **Desert plain**

Famous Sharons: **Osbourne, Gless, Stone**

Sharon's mission is to prepare a diverse selection of teachers and instructors for a career of rigorous disappointment.

She aims to achieve her goal by creating a Sharon-centered environment that unites her with other students through intimidation, both physically and mentally. Sharon is in control of the classroom. If she so chooses she will give up control, but only upon receiving first and last payment, cash only, no personal checks. Substitutes are her bread and butter, and out of the last twenty substitutes to visit her class, only one has made it through an entire school day without crying. Sharon is confident that she will not make it to graduation, and she looks forward to a long career in Food and Beverage Management.

S

TOBIN

Origin: **Hebrew**

Meaning: **Believing the Lord is good**

Famous Tobins: **Bell, Rote**

There's always going to be something about the way Tobin speaks that makes people uneasy.

He'll indulge in using too many pauses, all of them punctuated with supercilious 'you sees' and 'am I right or am I rights.' At first Tobin will seem like the perfect little prodigy, always on point with a foolproof observation or witty piece of quotable dialogue. Then he'll start wearing foreign-looking shoes and speaking with an unidentifiable accent. It won't be long before someone, maybe you, is going to want to tell Tobin that he needs to have his head stuck in the garbage can. Tobin may take this as a call to arms and put up his dukes. Don't flinch. Just repeat what you said about wanting to stick his head in the garbage can and everything should be alright.

TAMMY

Origin: **Aramaic**

Meaning: **Twin**

Famous Tammys: **Wynette, Faye**

Take the name Tammy and put it under a microscope. If you look closely you will see that the name, in its embryonic form, is riddled with moles.

Now there's a good chance that a girl born with the name Tammy will only have moles on her back, but it's possible that she may have moles on the soles of her feet. In that case, removal becomes not only very expensive, but very painful. At the present time it is not illegal to name your daughter Tammy, but some have ethical concerns, and it is possible that in the future there will be some kind of movement demanding there be legislature outlawing the name. It's a quality of life issue. Which side are you on?

T

UPTON

Origin: **Anglo-Saxon**

Meaning: **From the high town**

Famous Uptons: **Sinclair**

Upton's not going to have a lot of friends.

With a name like that, how can anyone relax? The name itself seems stitched out of tweed. It's hard to say the name Upton without feeling you've implicated yourself in a class struggle. The way your jaw clenches when you say the name makes you feel like it's you who's the snob.

URSULA

Origin: **Latin**

Meaning: **Little bear**

Famous Ursulas: **Andress, Le Guin**

Ursula is a minor name, never to be a major name, at least not with the people that count, a group of twelve men and twelve women known as The Tastemakers.

Working out of a loft in a newly gentrified part of the city, they spend most of the day trying to come up with a new name for the blighted, bombed-out six-block radius they have invaded with their trust funds and art school cred. So far they have come up with WesMo, Woodonica, and Fort Sunshine. When asked whether or not it was cool to name a little girl Ursua, they replied, *"We don't know. We haven't decided yet. But when we do we'll make sure to tell you after it's too late."*

U

VAL

Origin: **Latin**

Meaning: **To be healthy**

Famous Vals: **Kilmer, Lewton**

Val likes your sister.

Sleeps in his car. He's just looking for something to do, and now he's at your house, throwing groceries out the window. You can tell him he's not allowed to do that, tell him he's not allowed to take your sister to the supermarket without your parent's permission, tell him he's not allowed to invite over his friends and that his friends are not allowed to sleep in your closet. Go ahead. Tell him there are rules and watch as he dances across your lawn, tears apart your bike, and howls at the moon before announcing that there are no new tales to tell while teasing out his ten-foot pompadour.

VANESSA

Origin: **Greek**

Meaning: **Butterfly**

Famous Vanessas: **Williams, Redgrave**

A pretty name for a pretty girl, so you better make sure that's what you have.

It doesn't make sense to name your daughter Vanessa and then have her feel inferior to her own name. Better make sure that you have a pretty little girl. The world would look a whole lot prettier if it would just let Vanessa give it a makeover. Not to say that the world isn't pretty. That's not what Vanessa is trying to say. It's just that it doesn't look as good as it could. The oceans aren't as blue as they should be and the mountains are seriously dry. Think about how much better the world would feel if it lost a little bit around the Equator. This is not supposed to be taken as an insult. She's only trying to help. Vanessa's just trying to be honest. She's not going to lie. Whatever pops into her head is going to assume a sound and exit her mouth. Some people don't appreciate this. However, it's Vanessa's gift to the world.

V

WAYNE

Origin: **English**

Meaning: **Wagon maker**

Famous Waynes: **Newton, Gretzky**

Wayne's just not quick enough. That idea to remake Smokey and the Bandit? That was Wayne's idea.

It had Wayne's name written all over it. Wayne swears he had the idea first. But he just didn't move quickly enough and then someone else had the same idea and now look at how excellent that other person's life is. This tends to happen a lot to Wayne. He thought it might be a good idea to ask everyone to slow down so he could catch up, but somebody else took that idea as well.

WENDY

Origin: **English**

Meaning: **White, fair, blessed**

Famous Wendys: **Wasserstein, (O.), Williams**

Dear Francis: Yes, it's true, all Wendy's are whiners.

That's not a myth. Name your daughter Wendy and be prepared to find out that there is something wrong with everything, like cashmere, which, according to Wendy, is just too soft and too comfortable. Wendy doesn't want to be too comfortable. It's boring to be so comfortable. She wants to be uncomfortable. Being uncomfortable is an absolute must. The more uncomfortable you are the more there is to complain about. Wendy doesn't see what's so funny. Why does everything always have to be so funny? Sometimes Wendy likes to be serious. But no one wants to be serious anymore. Only Wendy.

The
only letter
of the alphabet
that,
on its own,
serves as a
warning.

Out of all the names you could name your child, why would you choose a name that starts with this letter? Is your son going to grow up to be a synthesizer repairman? Do you really want your daughter serving mixed cocktails at some South Florida Jai-alai palace? The Baby Boomers had no interest in their children being more successful than they were. It's time to break the cycle. Please move forward to the next letter.

YITZHAK

Origin: **Hebrew**

Meaning: **He will laugh**

Famous Yitzhaks: **Perlman, Rabin**

Yitzhak spends every single recess by himself, wandering around the blacktop, shoes untied.

There are rules he will not adhere to, and one of them is that no child is allowed to enter any classroom with untied shoes. Yitzhak knows this, yet he refuses to tie his shoes, which means that maybe he doesn't know how to ties his shoes, and he should, because someone has show him how to do it many, many times. He's also been told that if he can't remember how to tie his shoes one of the other children will help him, all he has to do is ask, but he won't, he'll just sit down and cry until someone does it for him, and most of the time it's one of the older children. They do it out of pity. They know Yitzhak won't say thank you, or even smile, these are not things he knows how to do. As a matter of fact, Yitzhak doesn't know if there's anything he knows how to do, even though his name implies that he might be great at something. There may be a chance this is true, but no one has seen any evidence of that yet. His mother says she has, but considering the source, it may be wise to just agree to disagree and leave it at that.

YVONNE

Origin: **French**

Meaning: **Yew**

Famous Yvonnes: **De Carlo, Craig**

Yvonne is an ugly name. It sounds like a rejected color, a cross between green and brown. Or it sounds like a disease you get from eating too much tapioca pudding. It sounds like a puddle of dirty water. I hear the name Yvonne and I think of a morbidly obese octogenarian locked in a cage wearing nothing but a checkerboard tablecloth. The name Yvonne is a horrowshow. No one under the age of 17 should be allowed to hear the name Yvonne without being accompanied by an adult. If it makes you feel better, keep telling yourself: IT'S ONLY A NAME. IT'S ONLY A NAME. IT'S ONLY A NAME.

ZACH

Origin: **Hebrew**

Meaning: **Pure**

Famous Zachs: **Braff, de la Rocha**

On more than one occasion Zach has been told that he's an insufferable twit, that the name Zach is actually synonymous with the term. However, Zach can't decide if he really is an insufferable twit. He has always assumed that he was a twit, but now he's not so sure about the insufferable part. Can a twit really be insufferable? Zach wants to know. He thinks that when you call someone a twit you are kind of already implying that they are past the point of being insufferable. Zach is not past the point of anything, ever. Don't you worry. He's just getting started even though it's close to the end.